May look cuddly but it's covered in bugs and algae.

The world's most

pointless*

~~wonderful~~ animals.

*or are they?

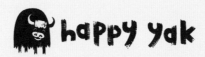 happy yak

For Leo.
P.B.

Aye-aye
← aficionado.

← A bit of a
prickly
character.

Quarto
Knows

Quarto is the authority on a wide range of topics.

Quarto educates, entertains and enriches the lives of our readers—enthusiasts and lovers of hands-on living.

www.quartoknows.com

↑
Sleeps
all day.

© 2021 Quarto Publishing plc
Text and illustration: © 2021 Philip Bunting
Concept by: Rhiannon Findlay

Never learned to read
← (but don't tell anyone).

Philip Bunting has asserted his right to be identified as the author and illustrator of this work.

Designers: Philip Bunting & Sarah Chapman-Suire
Senior Editor: Carly Madden ← Can't spell.
Creative Director: Malena Stojic
Associate Publisher: Rhiannon Findlay ← Guinea pig enthusiast.

First published in 2021 by Happy Yak, an imprint of The Quarto Group.
26391 Crown Valley Parkway, Suite 220, Mission Viejo, CA 92691, USA.
T: +1 949 380 7510 F: +1 949 380 7575
www.QuartoKnows.com

A CIP record for this book is available from the Library of Congress.

ISBN 978 0 7112 6241 6

Manufactured in Guangzhou, China EB042021

9 8 7 6 5 4 3 2 1

No vocal →
cords.

FSC
www.fsc.org
MIX
Paper from
responsible sources
FSC® C124385

Contents.

Shrewd
expression.

Kleptomaniac!

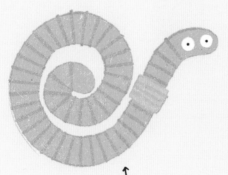

Heartless
mud muncher.

Bird
brain.

Not a real
unicorn.

Introduction.

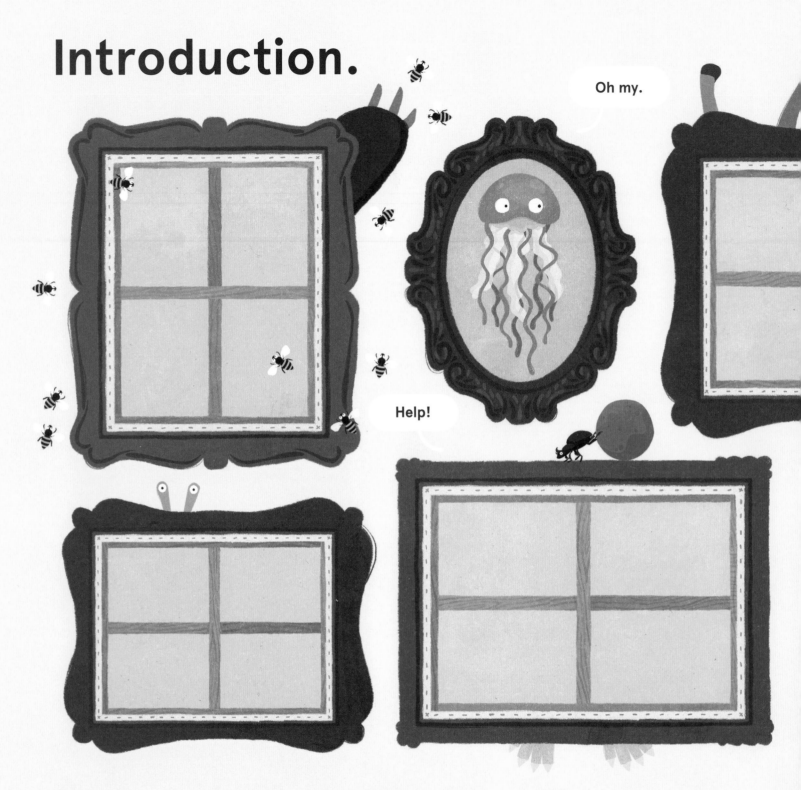

"To a person uninstructed in natural history, their country or seaside stroll is a walk through a gallery filled with wonderful works of art, nine-tenths of which have their faces turned to the wall." So said English biologist, Thomas Huxley.

The natural world is filled with countless wild and wonderful creatures of all shapes and species. Every animal on our planet—from aardvarks to zooplankton—has perfectly adapted over generations, to survive and ultimately thrive in its own unique environment.

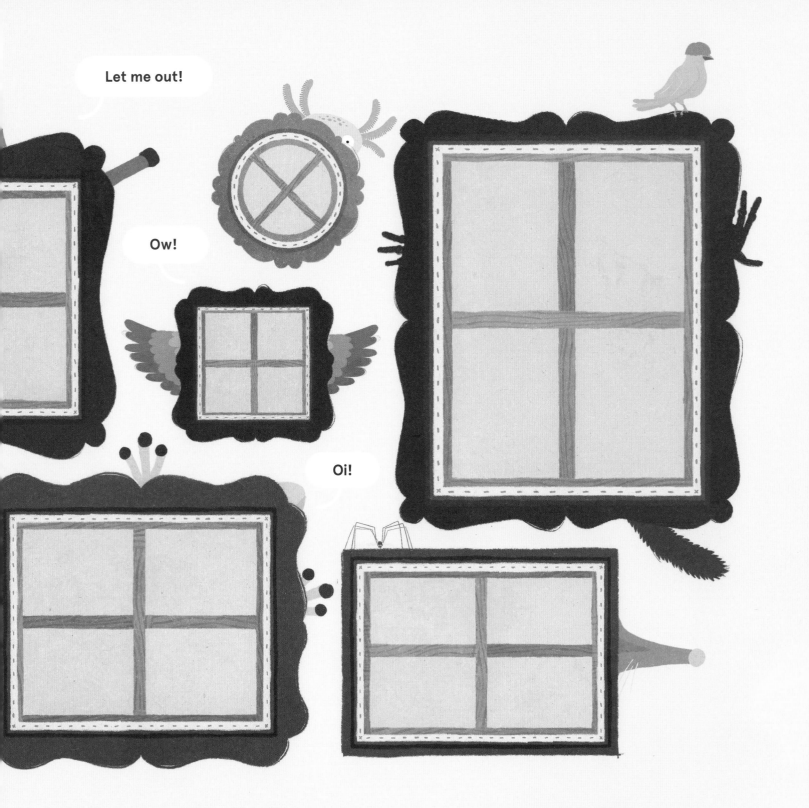

In turn, each ecosystem has adapted to thrive side-by-side with its remarkable residents. Our world is one beautifully balanced being, and we are all individual expressions of the same unknowable force. Each creature is an illustration of Darwinian evolution, and every animal has a unique yet important role to play on our precious planet. Even snails? Who said that? Anyway, let's meet just a few of the millions of species of wondrous wildlife that ~~make our marvelous world go round.~~ have no point whatsoever. Hey! Are you going to do this all the way through?

Jellyfish.

~~Medusozoa.~~

Wibblious wobblious ouchii.

Do not eat with custard.

Jello, sailor!

No brain.

No heart.

No bones.

← No eyes (yes, I know...).

← No nose.

No jellybutton.

Jellyfish are around **95% water.** Very similar to a bag **of soup.**

Jellyfish **eat** fish, crustaceans, algae, and plants— and then **poop** it all **out** of the **same hole.** Yep, its **mouth** is also its **butt.** Nom nom nom.

Some say they may be closely related to noodles.

Despite appearances, this diverse family of jolly wobblers are some of the most successful animals on our planet:

They live in every corner of the ocean.

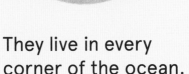
Where jellyfish are.
Where jellyfish aren't.

Scientists estimate that there could be as many as 300,000 species of jellyfish, but only 2,000 have been found so far. They have been here for at least 500,000,000 years (that's a lot longer than us!).

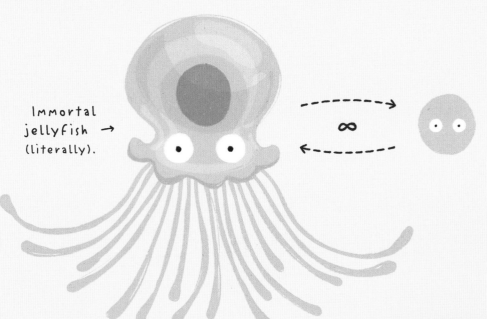

Immortal jellyfish → (literally).

∞

Some jellies may be able to live forever! Immortal jellyfish can return to a juvenile state if the going gets a little rough. Others, such as moon jellyfish, can even clone themselves.

To a sea turtle, a jellyfish is like a big bowl of wobbly jelly. Delicious! However, there is one particularly aggressive species of giant jellyfish called the "pink meanie," who is not to be trifled with.

Quokka.

~~Setonix brachyurus.~~

Pukesinmouth notsocutius.

Quokkas "smile" because they're hot, and pant to cool down. They are not being friendly.

Throws up in its own mouth, → then eats it.

Tiny, chubby pseudo-roo. →

Will chomp you, given half a chance.

Secretly despises selfies (only interested in your snacks).

Heart of stone.

Will shriek like an undignified banshee if attacked.

Warm and fuzzy on the outside, cold and ruthless on the inside.

Native to a few small pockets of southwestern Australia, quokkas are wonderfully adapted to their dry, sun-baked environment. Able to climb trees, eat bark, and go for up to a month without water, these mini macropods (a type of marsupial—an animal that carries its young in a pouch) are true survivalists. Due to their nutrient-poor diet, quokkas eat each meal twice (swallowing once, before part-digesting and regurgitating), in order to extract as much good stuff as they can from each mouthful.

Pigeon.

~~Columba livia.~~

Rattus wingus.

Slowly but surely **taking over the** great town squares of the world.

Breadcrumb connoisseur.

Bird brain.

Head bobs when it walks.

A bit cooey.

No respect for statues.

Creepy, scaly toes.

Loves to poop on anything in reach!

Why don't you ever see baby pigeons? They're up to something...

These city-dwelling superbirds have lived alongside us in our towns and cities for at least 6,500 years. Pigeons are one of the few animals in the world that have the ability to recognize themselves in the mirror, a marker of profound intelligence, shared only with a few apes (including you and I), dolphins, elephants, and a handful of cocky parrots. As well as being incredibly smart, they are also one of the fastest birds in the world, clocking speeds of up to 93 miles (149 km) per hour!

Myotonic goat.

~~Capra aegagrus hircus.~~

Scaredius stiffus.

Also known as "Tennessee stiff-legs" ...and "fainting goat."

Somebody should teach them about the fight-or-flight response.

Unwilling participant in many funny animal videos.

Not so gruff.
↓

Word of advice: never throw a surprise party for a myotonic goat.

Very nervous (terrible public speaker).

Grows a goatee to try to look tough. Fail.

Goats are some of the hardiest and most nimble creatures in the animal kingdom, able to scale sheer cliffs and eat just about anything with roots and leaves. But this particular breed is famous for another reason. When startled—say by an unruly dog or a breakdancing farmer— a myotonic goat's muscles will immediately tense up, causing the goat to fall to the ground as if it has fainted. During these brief episodes, the goats don't lose consciousness, and are typically back on their feet within seconds...until the next time they get a fright.

Leech.

~~Hirudinea.~~

Suckus majorus.

Most species have three jaws. A dentist's nightmare.

300 tiny but terrifyingly sharp teeth.

Pretty much **blind.**

Completely deaf.

Literally sucks the blood from other animals, like a slimy vampire.

Aaaaaah!

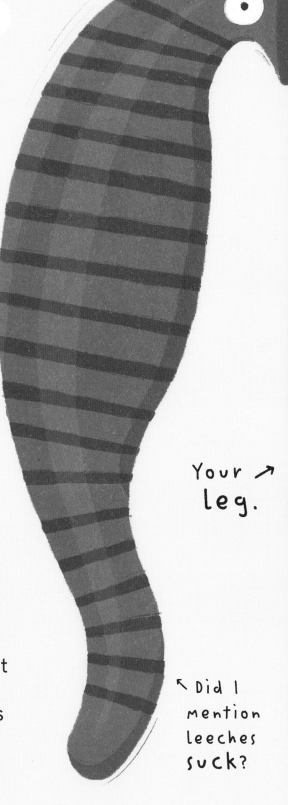

Your **leg.**

← Did I mention leeches suck?

Leeches are highly successful little suckers—there are over 650 species that exist on every continent, except Antarctica. Not all leech species suck blood, but those that do can drink up to five times their own bodyweight in the red stuff. While they may not look too smart, a leech has 32 brains! And their nervous system is considered so similar to ours, that leeches are often used by doctors to help improve blood circulation in humans.

Dung beetle.

~~Scarabaeidae.~~

Rolliae poliae poopiae.

Elephant poop*
(actual size).
↓

Some live
in poop!
↓

Eats
poop!
↓

Loves
poop!
↓

Has **wings**, but
prefers to pedal
poop. Honestly...
↓

No nose,
fortunately.
↓

↖
Dung beetles do
not take heed of
the old saying
"you are what
you **eat**."

↑
Hairy legs.

There are around 8,000 species of dung beetle on our poop-popping planet, and they can be found on every continent, except Antarctica. All dung beetles love to eat poop. Nasty. These fecal fiends eat, move, bury, and even live inside the droppings of other animals—helping to keep our soils healthy in the process. You see, when an animal digests its dinner, it won't typically extract all of the nutrients from its meal. Dung beetles are finely tuned to find the nutritious bits in any poop.

Dung beetles are great navigators. Just as moths use the moon to find their way at night, dung beetles use the bright strip of stars in the Milky Way to orient themselves.

Dung beetles are the world's strongest animal, relative to their weight. Some can pull a poo over 1,100 times their own weight—that's like you pulling along 12 African elephants!

*Artist's impression only. You try drawing one.

↑
Dung beetles prefer herbivore plop, for its top notes of corn and nutty aftertaste.

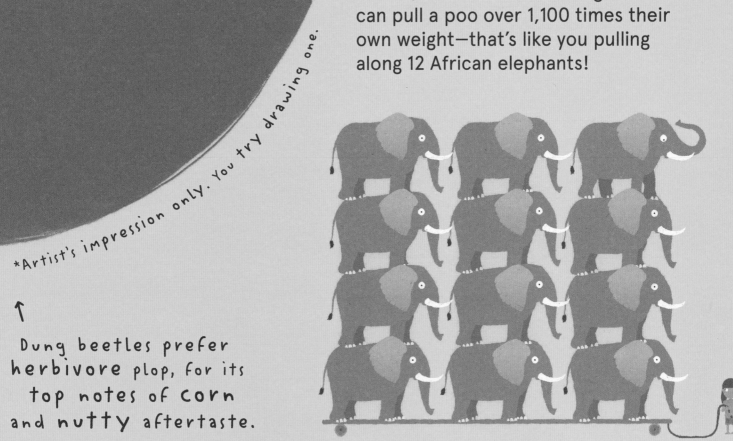

Don't try this at home.

Blobfish.

~~Psychrolutes marcidus.~~ Blancmangea blancmangea.

Just **look** at it.

Related to a
fishy family
called
fatheads.

No bones
(hence the
blobbyness).

Can't do
sit-ups
(no muscles).

Can't hunt,
due to a
lack of
muscles.

Dejected
expression.

↑
A great **face** for **radio.**
Unfortunately, most electronics
don't work on the ocean floor.

No teeth
(but wouldn't brush
them anyway).

Blobfish are unfairly renowned as one of the ugliest creatures around. They live deep in the oceans around Australia and New Zealand, spending their entire life hovering just above the sea floor, hoovering up crustaceans, plankton, and other deep-sea delicacies. Because of their extreme environment, there's still a lot we don't know, like how long they live or how they reproduce. But because we know *where* they live, we do know that their only enemies are humans (especially those with deep-sea fishing nets or a cruel sense of humor).

Blobfish live at depths of between 1,970–3,940 feet (600–1,200 m) where the atmospheric pressure is up to 120 times greater than it is at sea level. In the deep-sea, high-pressure environment that they have evolved to thrive in, blobfish actually look pretty typically fishy.

In the deep:
more fishy,
less blobby.

With spongy flesh and no bones, blobfish are perfectly adapted to this extreme environment. At these depths, our bony, land-loving human bodies would instantly be squished under the pressure! The reverse goes for blobfish, when they are removed from their natural habitat. At sea level, their blobby bodies can't adjust to the change in pressure—and so they quickly deform.

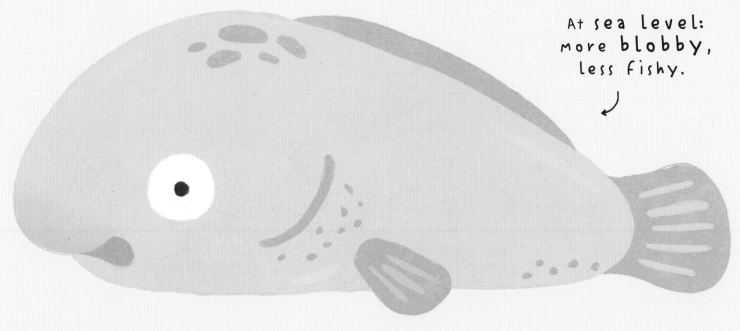

At sea level:
more blobby,
less fishy.

Sun bear.

~~Helarctos malayanus.~~
Littlus teddis.

Small bear complex.
↓

AKA "Dog Bear." Sounds cute, but you wouldn't take one for a walk.

Sun bears are omnivorous, but their favorite snack can pack a bit of a sting.

Poor eyesight. →

Does not hibernate. →
(Must get a bit grizzly.)

Buzz off!

← Ridiculously long tongue (around 10 inches or 25 cm)! Not great with tongue-twisters.

Terrible table → manners.

While walking on all fours, the world's smallest species of bear would only reach to an adult human's hip. Despite its bright name, the sun bear typically sleeps through the day and is most active at night. Its name comes from a golden patch on its chest and neck, which is said to represent the rising sun. Each bear's patch is unique—similar to our fingerprints!

Red-lipped batfish.

~~Ogeocephalus darwini.~~

Poutus snoutus.

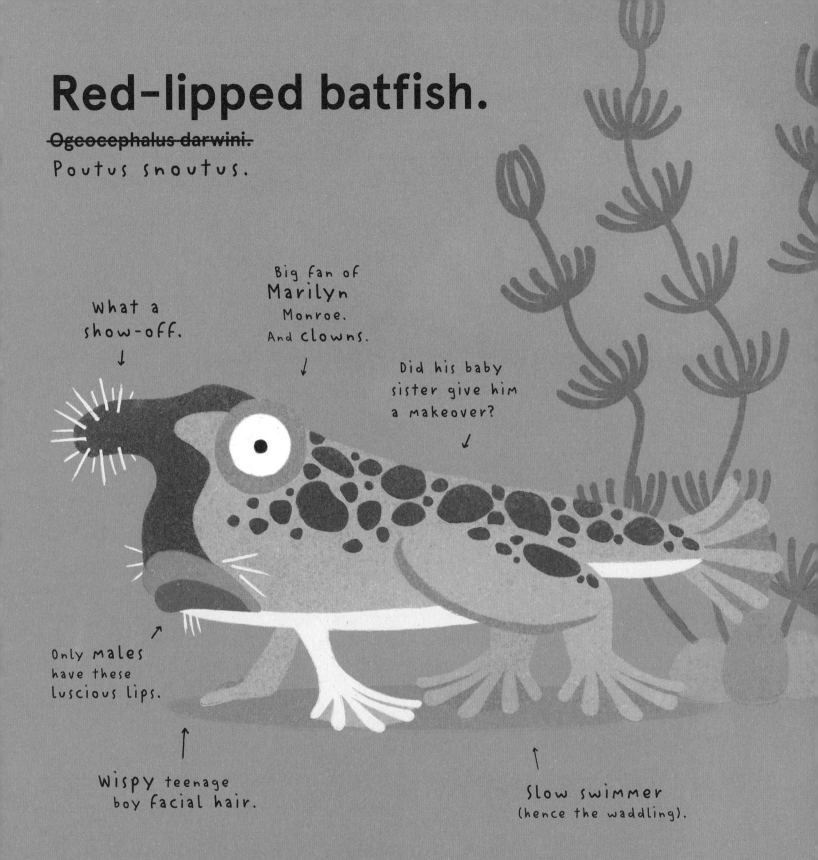

What a
show-off.
↓

Big fan of
Marilyn
Monroe.
And clowns.
↓

Did his baby
sister give him
a makeover?
↓

Only males
have these
luscious lips.
↗

Wispy teenage
boy facial hair.
↑

Slow swimmer
(hence the waddling).
↑

Commonly found waddling along the ocean floor around the Galapagos Islands, these voracious carnivores have many wonderful adaptations to their life on the seabed. Beyond the males' vibrant red lips (which are used to attract a mate), all red-lipped batfish have developed pectoral and pelvic fins capable of walking on the sea floor. In fact, they are so well adapted to walking that they rarely swim.

Cicada.

~~Cicadoidea.~~

Waitiae-waitiae flappi-flappi-buzz-
buzz-flappi-flappi-buzz... deadus.

(Not tic tacs®.)
Eggs hatch after
around 10 weeks.

Nymphs are born
free but choose
to quickly dig
below ground.

A bit
wasteful.

Lives underground
for up to
17 years!

This family of over 3,000 species can be recognized by their stocky
bodies and relatively large heads. All cicadas fit into one of two groups –
annual cicadas or periodical cicadas. While annual cicadas appear every
summer, periodical cicadas live underground as nymphs, before they
emerge as fully fledged flying adults.

Adult periodical cicadas lay their eggs in tiny holes they make in branches or twigs. After about 10 weeks, the eggs hatch into small, wingless nymphs, which fall from the plant and quickly dig below the ground. These cidadas-in-waiting will live below the ground for up to 17 years, feeding on sap they suck up from tree roots.

Excessively noisy!

Big head!

Adult cicadas only live for a few weeks.

Lives 99% of life underground. Someone should tell them what they're missing out on.

When seeking a mate, adult males make a buzzing, screeching sound that can be louder than a motorbike!

When it's eventually time to emerge, the nymph will wait for the soil to reach 64°F (18°C) before digging its way above ground. The nymph will typically climb a tree trunk and shed its skin, emerging as a winged adult cicada. The cicada will then fly off to mate, leaving its old nymphy skin behind. Adult females will lay up to 600 eggs, before dropping dead after just a few sweet weeks in the open air.

Goldfish.

~~Carassius auratus.~~
Tedious domesticus.

Terrible pet.

Can't fetch a stick.

Refuses to purr.

Won't do tricks.

You can't cuddle a goldfish.

What does it do? ↓

Will eat any fish that fits in its mouth. Would eat you if it could.

Can't blink (no eyelids).

Will turn white if left in the dark!

Eats its own poop. Probably.

We humans have kept goldfish for thousands of years. But think carefully before you commit to a goldfish as a pet, as they have been known to live into their mid-40s! They have an amazing sixth sense (a combination of hearing, touch, and balance), which helps the fish to sense vibrations in water, alerting the goldfish to both predators and prey. And contrary to popular myth, recent studies have shown that goldfish can retain memories for at least 6 months!

Stick insect.

~~Phasmatodea.~~

Twigeous walkie walkie.

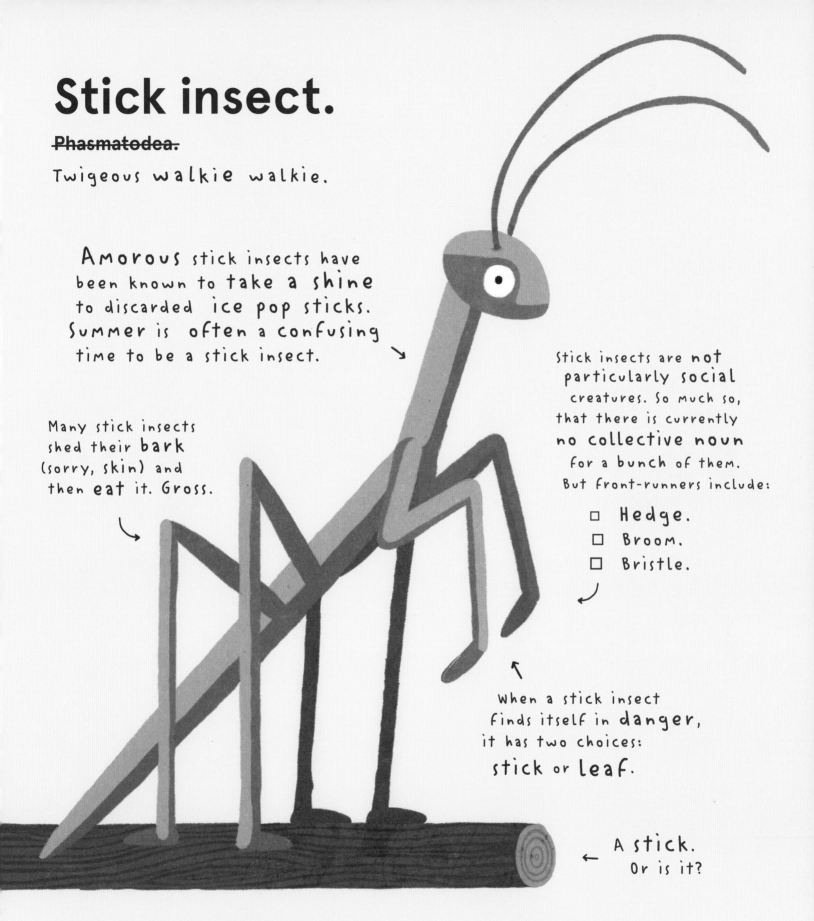

Amorous stick insects have been known to take a shine to discarded ice pop sticks. Summer is often a confusing time to be a stick insect.

Many stick insects shed their **bark** (sorry, skin) and then **eat** it. Gross.

Stick insects are **not** particularly **social** creatures. So much so, that there is currently **no collective noun** for a bunch of them. But front-runners include:

☐ **Hedge.**
☐ Broom.
☐ Bristle.

When a stick insect finds itself in **danger**, it has two choices: **stick** or **leaf.**

A **stick.**
Or is it?

There are over 3,000 species of stick insect on the tree of life. Each type has branched out to closely resemble their surroundings in both shape and color. Even stick insect eggs have evolved to mimic seeds, making these walking sticks some of the best-camouflaged creatures on the planet.

Earthworm.

~~Lumbricus terrestris.~~

Squiggleous wriggleous.

No bones.

Gross!

Gross. →

So gross.

No eyes in real life.

Gross. →

The collective noun for a group of earthworms is a "clew" (with an emphasis on the "ew").

Gross.

Heartless mud munchers!
Earthworms don't have a heart, rather they have five heart-like pumps called aortic arches.

Fun fact: if you **cut a worm in half** you don't get two worms, just **one** very **dead** worm.

Earthworms live all around the world; they can be found anywhere where there is moist soil, but they are most common in wet or forested areas. They can vary in size, growing up to 6.5 feet (2 m) in some parts of Australia!

← Please do not try this at home.

22

Moist soil is a must for earthworms, as they do not have lungs. Instead they absorb oxygen through their skin. And their skin must stay moist to allow the oxygen to move into their bloodstream.

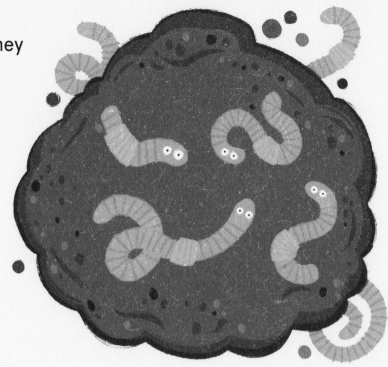

Charles Darwin

The Formation of Vegetable Mould Through the Action of Worms

Charles Darwin loved earthworms. He wrote an entire book about them in 1881, in which he said, "Worms have played a more important part in the history of the world than some people would at first suppose."

I preferred The Very Hungry Caterpillar.

By munching their way through soil, earthworms move minerals and nutrients around, helping plants to thrive. Without plants, there would be no life on land. Without soil, there would be no plants. No soil, no you!

Naked mole-rat.

~~Heterocephalus glaber.~~

Toothus wrinklesausage.

Sleeps in piles of other naked mole-rats (to stay warm).

Not a mole. Not a rat. But most definitely naked.

Almost deaf. What?

Pretty much blind.

Weird, wormy tail.

Eats its own poop. Of course it does.

Teeth move independently, like chopsticks!

Grinds its teeth when sleeping, like many humans.

These subterranean squeakers are perfectly adapted for their life below ground. With over one quarter of their muscle mass in their jaws, naked mole-rats chomp complex tunnel systems that can stretch over many miles and can house hundreds of individuals. Unlike other mammals, they live in colonies where each mole-rat has a special role to play—and whether that be queen, soldier, or worker, each individual plays their part for the good of the group.

Inca tern.

~~Larosterna inca.~~

Mustacheo bandito.

Classic bandit appearance.

Steals food from fellow sea creatures!

Strange cat-like "meow" call.

A confident (some would say cocky) bird.

Elaborate moustache, primarily for the purpose of showing-off.

They will steal other birds' nests— quite fond of roosting in Humboldt penguins' nests.

Not great in the water due to relatively small feet.

Inca terns are so agile and confident in the air, that they have been known to swoop and take fish from the mouths of unsuspecting sea lions! They will also pinch scraps from passing fishing trawlers. In both male and female inca terns their moustache-like plumage develops by the time they are around two years old. This fancy facial feature is an indicator of health—the longer the plumage, the better the health of the bird. So birds with the most elaborate moustaches tend to produce the most babies.

Groundhog.

~~Marmota monax.~~

Meteorologist terrapiggius.

A bit of a
← pest (steals
crops).

Lives down
a hole.
↓

Also known as woodchucks, landbeavers, and whistlepigs (adorable!), groundhogs live in underground tunnel networks that can stretch over 50 feet (20 m), with special chambers for sleeping and going to the bathroom. They use these burrows to raise their young, hide from predators, and hibernate through the winter.

Fast **asleep** for roughly three months every year. **Lazy**.

Groundhogs are the largest member of the sciuridae family, which also includes squirrels. Despite their preference for the subterranean life, groundhogs can climb trees to escape a pesky predator! And they are excellent swimmers, if pushed.

↑
Excessively windy (thanks to all of those root vegetables).

Groundhogs know exactly when to emerge from their winter hibernation, to give their little ones the best chance of survival—they have impeccable timing. So much so they've even been used to predict the coming of spring in parts of North America.

A bit nosy.
↓

↖
Do not trust this rotund rodent to predict the **weather**. Always consult a proper meteorologist.

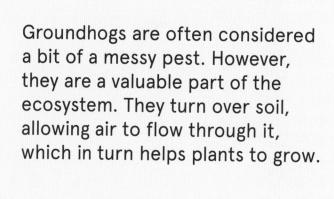

Groundhogs are often considered a bit of a messy pest. However, they are a valuable part of the ecosystem. They turn over soil, allowing air to flow through it, which in turn helps plants to grow.

Sea urchin.

~~Echinoidea.~~

Littlus priccus.

No brain.

Its bum is on top of its head, like a stinky blowhole.

Many species are **venomous**, and most are very **prickly**.

No eyes
(Yes, yes...).

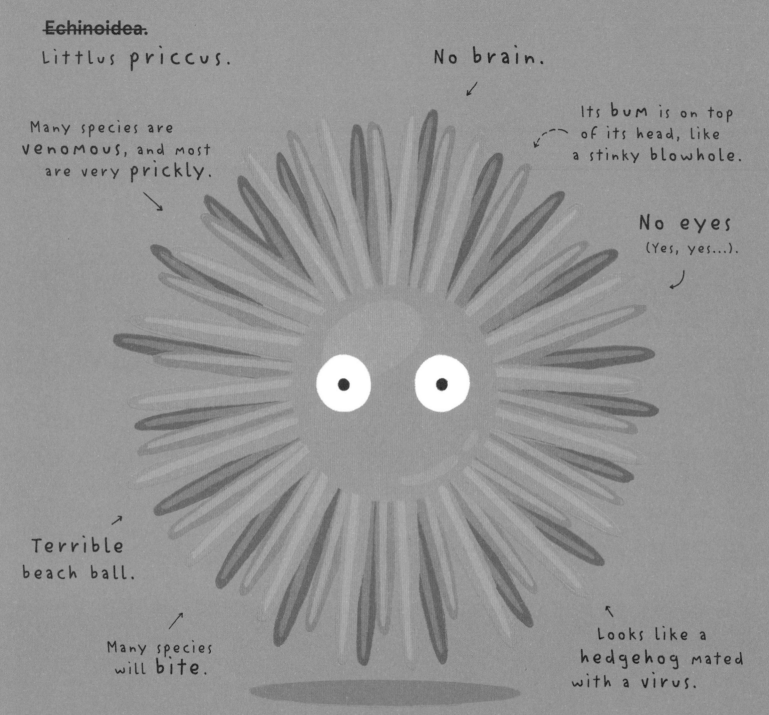

Terrible beach ball.

Many species will **bite**.

Looks like a hedgehog mated with a virus.

These spiny seafaring rascals are close relatives of starfish and sea cucumbers. They are omnivorous and will clean up just about anything that will fit in their strange mouth. This odd mouth is equipped with five sharp teeth that can bite through rock! Urchins play a critical role in maintaining the balance between coral and algae in coral reef ecosystems. Elsewhere, they are the favored food of many creatures—including sea otters, fish, sea birds, and even sometimes humans.

Koala.

~~Phascolarctos cinereus.~~

Notabear sleepi sleepi.

Most definitely **not a bear.**

Only eats tough, **TOXIC** eucalyptus leaves that would finish off most mammals! Weirdos.

Poor eyesight.

Feeds its own **poop** to its babies.

Sleeps most of the day.

Koala fingerprints are so similar to humans that there has been confusion at crime scenes!

Your average koala will spend up to 18 hours each day fast asleep. Their poor diet of toxic eucalyptus leaves causes them to feel a little tired and a bit grouchy. When koala babies (joeys) are born, they do not have the gut bacteria required to digest the poisonous plants. But never fear, koala moms make great cooks! When a joey is ready to eat solid food, its mom will feed it her own poop (also known as pap), to gently introduce good bacteria to her baby's guts.

Platypus.

~~Ornithorhynchus anatinus.~~ Mammalia duckfaceus weirdus.

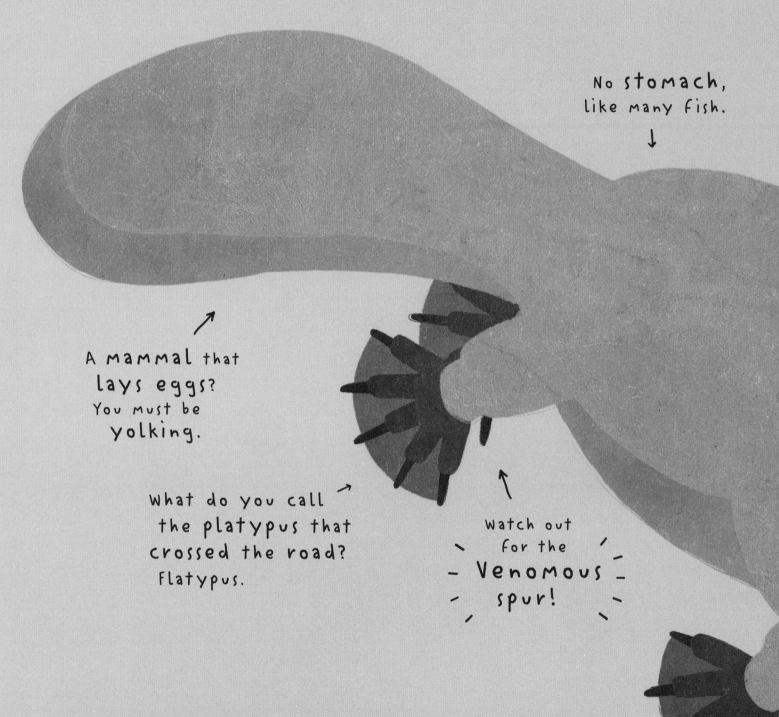

No stomach,
like many fish.
↓

A mammal that
lays eggs?
You must be
yolking.

What do you call
the platypus that
crossed the road?
Flatypus.

Watch out
for the
Venomous
spur!

Weird
toes.

When biologists first sent a platypus skin to London from
Australia, in the late 1700s, the recipients thought it was
a hoax. This freshwater mammal has a body and coat a
little like an otter, webbed toes, a soft leathery bill, and
no stomach! The males have a venomous spur on their back
legs, and the females lay eggs. A rare creature indeed.

Platypuses are thought to have first appeared 110-120 million years ago, not long after mammals evolved from reptiles. Just like reptiles, platypuses lay eggs, rather than give birth to live young, like other mammals do. They belong to a very special family of mammals called monotremes, which includes only platypuses and echidnas.

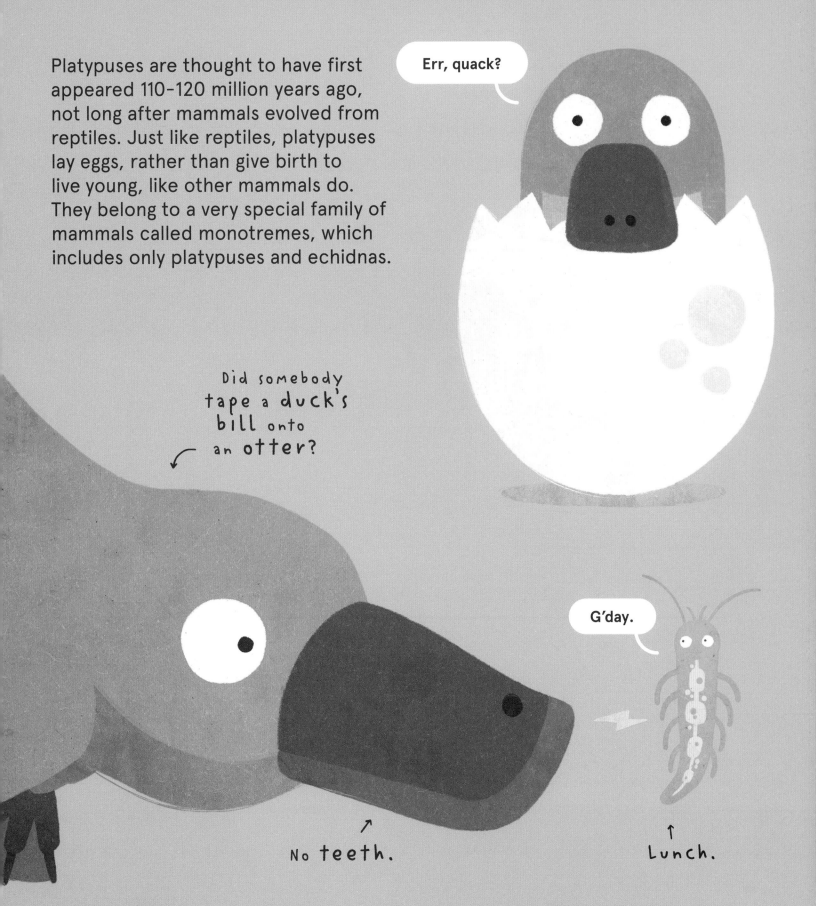

Err, quack?

Did somebody tape a duck's bill onto an otter?

No teeth.

G'day.

Lunch.

Their unique bill can detect tiny electric fields generated by living things in the water—a process known as electrolocation—which the platypus uses to hunt small fish and crustaceans.

Ostrich.

~~Struthio camelus.~~

Biggus chiccus.

Tiny brain! →
An ostrich's brain is smaller than its eye.

No teeth!
Ostriches swallow small rocks to help break down food.*

Built-in feather dusters.

Can't fly.

Extra-long chomp zone for predators to aim for.

*Poops are no fun for this big bird.

Ostriches lay the largest eggs in the world, weighing up to an eye-watering 13.3 pounds (1.5 kg). Oof.

Only two toes (per foot)! Most birds have three or four toes.

To avoid becoming fast food out on the African savannah, the largest and heaviest bird on Earth can run at speeds of up to 43 miles (70 km) per hour, using its wings as rudders to outmanoeuvre predators. However, if they can't run away, another defense tactic an ostrich uses is to flop their neck to the ground and freeze, with their head perfectly flat on the ground in front of them. From a distance, this makes the hiding ostrich harder for predators to spot. To us, it looks like they've buried their head in the sand, hence the popular myth.

Inland taipan.

~~Oxyuranus microlepidotus.~~

Bitaebitae deadsedeadse.

Luckily for us, the world's most venomous snake prefers the quiet life—choosing to hang out in the sparsely populated Australian outback, where human interaction is relatively rare. Taipan venom is so potent that it can kill an adult human within 30 minutes. Alarmingly, your average inland taipan holds enough venom at any one time to take down 100 adult humans.

↑
what happens if it accidentally bites its own tongue?

Probably not the best choice of pet.

Bad attitude (also known as the "fierce snake").

↑
No warning rattle.

Does it really need quite so much venom?

← No arms. →
Or legs.

If this snake bites you, you are hissstory.

Guinea pig.

~~Cavia porcellus.~~

Squeakius fuzzballi.

Doesn't come from Guinea...

...or Papua New Guinea.

And isn't related to pigs.

↑ Teeth never stop growing.

Four toes up front.

← Odd number of toes. →

Three toes down the back.

No tail! No tail? Pah! What kind of mammal is this?

Guinea pigs make great pets. They are very social little creatures, and will often purr when they are happy (or scared) and jump around when they are excited, an exercise known as 'popcorning'! Some guinea pig squeaks are ultrasonic—reaching frequencies above 20,000 Hz (humans can only hear sounds up to about 20,000 Hz).

Guinea pigs originated in the Andes (South America), where the locals believe that they can help to cure a whole bunch of human illnesses. Typical Andean guinea pig treatments range from rubbing the poor little pigs on the affected area, to eating them! In fact, the guinea pig is a popular dish in many South American countries, including Peru, Bolivia, Ecuador, and Colombia.

Andean roast ham.
✓

While we generally prefer our guinea pigs as pets rather than palate cleansers, they have also been used in western medicine. Guinea pigs share an odd evolutionary quirk with us humans—the inability to produce vitamin C—which has made them our traditional testing subject for many modern medicines. Hence the popular term "guinea pig" to describe a test subject.

Mayfly.

~~Ephemeroptera.~~

Hereus todayus gonus tomorrus.

Of the 3,000+ species of mayfly, only a handful actually emerge in May.

In their winged adult form, most species live for less than a day. Some only last a few minutes!

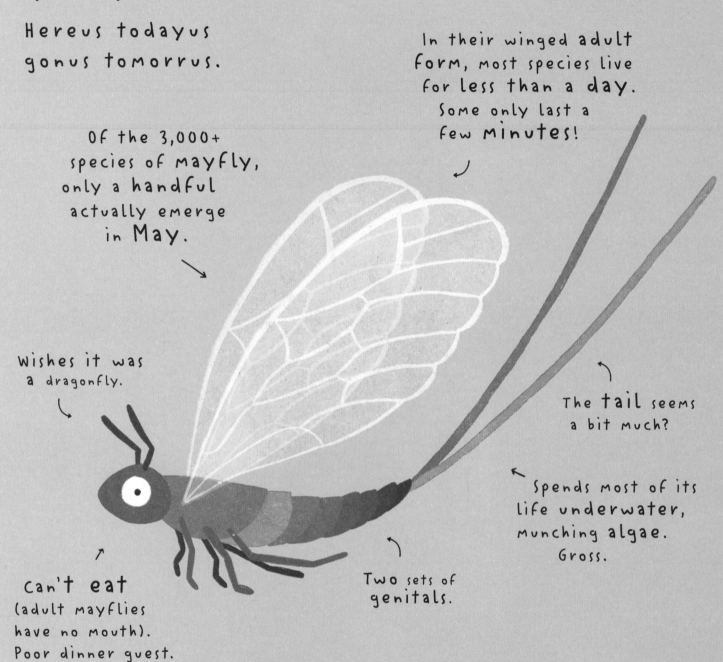

Wishes it was a dragonfly.

The tail seems a bit much?

Spends most of its life underwater, munching algae. Gross.

Can't eat (adult mayflies have no mouth). Poor dinner guest.

Two sets of genitals.

During their short life, a mayfly will go through four stages: egg (lasting a few weeks), larval stage (lasting a few months to two years), sub-imago (lasting minutes to a few days), and the adult stage (imago), which lasts between a few minutes and a few days, depending upon the species. As adults, their only goal is to reproduce. As soon as their mayfly-making mission is accomplished—and the next generation of eggs are laid—the adult mayflies quite simply drop dead!

Striped skunk.

~~Mephitis mephitis.~~

Anus horribilis.

Skunk stink is **highly flammable,** making them a highly questionable choice of guest at a barbecue, campfire, or **birthday** party.

A skunk's funk is **so potent** that it can cause **temporary blindness!**

Terrible eyesight. →

An ironically excellent sense of smell.

→ 15-foot (4.5-m) blast zone!

← Short legs and mediocre claws.

Skunks don't want to spray you with their posterior perfume, but they can, and they will. Their malodorous mist is the skunk's only real defense against predators. Fortunately, these are well-mannered little mammals and they will give you fair notice before letting one rip. A skunk often performs a little pre-pong warning dance, which can include growls, shakes, stomps, and even a little handstand!

Giant anteater.

~~Myrmecophaga tridactyla.~~

Hooversnouteous antnomnomeous ginormea.

As their name suggests, giant anteaters eat enormous quantities of ants—up to 35,000 ants or termites in a single day! They use their long, skinny, sticky tongues to poke inside ant hills or termite mounds to gobble up as many insects as possible—hundreds per minute—before the ants begin to bite back!

Poor hearing. ↓

Shoddy eyesight (very near-sighted). ↘

Argh! Turn back!

Look at that honker! ↓

No teeth! (Swallows ants whole.) Rude.

24-inch-long (60-cm) tongue, covered in super-sticky saliva.

Anteaters are gracious and respectful hunters. They will be careful to take only as many ants as they need and will never destroy a colony, leaving enough ants to rebuild. This way the anteater will never run out of food.

How considerate.

Uh-oh.

↑
Number twos must be a bit scratchy with all of that crunchy exoskeletal ant fiber.

↑
Could do with a trim.

Anteater claws are huge—around 4 inches (10 cm) long—and ideal for digging into ant hills. These claws also come in handy when fending off predators, such as a jaguar. If an anteater feels threatened, it can stand up on its hind legs and slash at its attacker with its front claws. Ouch!

Gloster canary.

Serinus canaria domesticus.

Hairyus canarius.

Gloster canaries are big fans of the early Beatles.

If your MOM tries to → give you a haircut like this, grab the bowl and run.

Not the best singer, despite being a canary.

This bird would not last long in the wild, as it cannot see where it is flying.

Can't talk like a parrot.

Can't play fetch.

Canaries have been kept as pets for centuries. Gloster canaries do not naturally occur in the wild— rather they are the product of selective breeding at the hands of humans.

The Gloster canary was first recognized as a breed in England in 1925. Today, they are still prized as pets for their cheerful nature and, of course, for their peculiar plumage.

Aye-aye.

~~Daubentonia madagascariensis.~~

Weirdus digitus maximus.

Creepy/cute feline facial features. ↓

Possibly named by a pirate, in honor of his beloved captain. ↓

Only found on Madagascar, but it's very bad luck if you see one there, → apparently.

Super-strange fishing rod finger (excellent booger retriever). ↖

Aye-ayes were first classified by scientists as rodents! How rude. →

Bushy tail, possibly stolen from a squirrel. ↳

Front teeth never stop growing, like a rat's. ↖

Aye-ayes are a primate, and are closely related to you! Can you see the family resemblance? ↳

Aye-ayes have a really long, slender finger on each hand. They use these to locate tasty insect larvae, by tapping on trees and feeling for the vibrations of bugs. Once they find them, the finger acts a bit like a fishing rod, to pluck the larvae out. Aye-ayes are believed to be the only primate that uses echolocation to hunt.

Only three digits per paw (obviously).

Can't fart and only poops once a week!

Completely color-blind.

May look cuddly but it's covered in bugs and algae.

Scratch
Scratch

Top speed: 10 feet (3 m) per minute!

Mother sloths give **birth** while hanging upside down!

Three-toed sloth.

~~Bradypus variegatus.~~ Slowcus pokeus.

The world's slowest mammal lives a famously lethargic lifestyle. But it's not laziness—life in the slow lane brings many advantages for the sloth. Keeping things slow and steady helps them to regulate their body temperature, as well as conserving energy and staying hidden from predators (such as jaguars).

Sloths are arboreal creatures, which means they spend their time in trees. They do everything up there, except one thing...poop! They go to the ground once a week to do a number two. This bumper bowel movement can weigh as much as one third of a sloth's bodyweight!

Sloths have an extra vertebra in their neck, which allows them to turn their head an impressive 360 degrees, giving them a super view of the forest around them. Another surprising superpower is their ability to swim up to three times faster than they can walk. Better still, sloths can hold their breath for up to 40 minutes!

Slow movement and a sloth's thick, wiry fur provide an attractive habitat for a plethora of bugs, grubs, and microorganisms. But these little hitchhikers aren't all bad news—many sloths sport a greenish tinge to their coats (thanks to colonies of algae), which gives them an extra layer of camouflage in their treetop home.

Daddy longlegs.

~~Tipulidae.~~

Incius wincius notaspider.

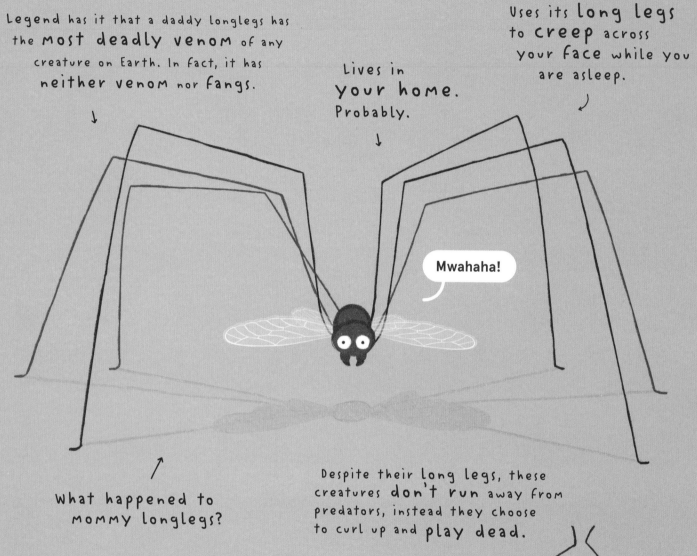

Legend has it that a daddy longlegs has the **most deadly venom** of any creature on Earth. In fact, it has **neither venom nor fangs.**

Lives in **your home.** Probably.

Uses its **long legs** to **creep** across your **face** while you are asleep.

Mwahaha!

What happened to **mommy longlegs?**

Despite their long legs, these creatures **don't run** away from predators, instead they choose to curl up and **play dead.**

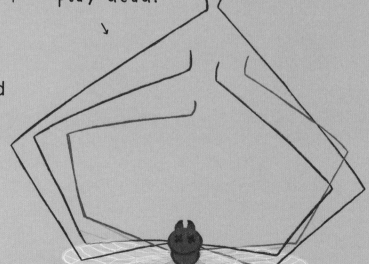

There are over 15,000 species of daddy longlegs (also known as crane flies) around the world. Despite popular belief, these spindly stalwarts of the animal kingdom are not venomous, nor can they bite or suck your blood. They are pretty harmless and provide a valuable source of food for birds on every continent, except Antarctica.

Silkie chicken.

~~Gallus domesticus.~~

Sixdigitus pompomface.

Unnecessarily **fluffy** plumage.

Blue-black colored **bones** (and the same color **meat** when cooked)!

Why did the silkie cross the road? Because it couldn't fly due to its puny wings and excessively fluffy feathers.

Fluffy feathers get very **soggy** (and smelly) in the rain.

Doesn't lay many eggs, compared to most chickens.

Silkies can sprout **five toes** per foot (chickens typically have only **four**). Ewww.

Silkies are one of the oldest known breeds of domestic chicken. Their skeleton and skin muscles are a blue-black color! This atypical coloring is due to a genetic quirk called fibromelanosis, where the body overproduces pigmentation, inside and out! These blue-black beauties are considered a delicacy in many parts of the world.

45

Pufferfish.

~~Tetraodontidae.~~

Veriverius defensivus.

A pufferfish packs enough **toxin** to finish off 30 adult humans! Seems a bit excessive.

Prickly little character.

Do not eat! Or it will be a fugu boo-boo (see right).

Slow, clumsy swimmer.

Puny fin.

Way too defensive.

If eaten with **chips**, make sure to order some **ta-ta sauce**.

The world's angriest party balloon.

Has four strange teeth that never stop growing.

There are over 120 species in the pufferfish family, but they are all relatively small in size and pretty slow. So to avoid being chomped by bigger fish, pufferfish have evolved the ability to suck huge amounts of water into their stretchy stomachs, inflating themselves to a diameter larger than most predators would dare to munch! But self-inflation is not the only defense technique in the pufferfish playbook...

Almost all pufferfish contain a toxin called tetrodotoxin, which makes them taste horrible and is deadly to pretty much any creature that takes a bite. Despite this, some pufferfish flesh—a tiny, non-toxic part called fugu—is a delicacy in Japan. Due to the risks involved, Japanese chefs must undertake three years of training in order to prepare it! However, there are still multiple fugu-induced deaths in Japan every year.

Fugu sashimi chart:

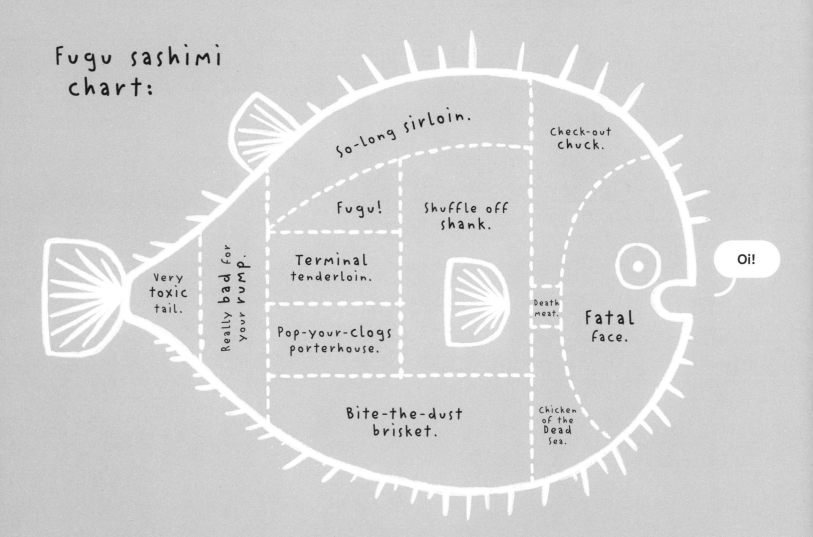

So-long sirloin.

Check-out chuck.

Very toxic tail.

Really bad for your rump.

Fugu!

Terminal tenderloin.

Shuffle off shank.

Pop-your-clogs porterhouse.

Death meat.

Fatal face.

Bite-the-dust brisket.

Chicken of the Dead Sea.

Oi!

Humans are strange creatures, but we're not the only mammals who like to tinker with toxic stuff. Dolphins deliberately play with pufferfish to get them to release their defensive toxins. In small doses, this has a hallucinogenic effect on the dolphins, which they appear to enjoy!

Giant panda.

~~Ailuropoda melanoleuca.~~

Bearius lazius.

Always looks **tired** but refuses to **hibernate** (like many human toddlers).

Can't **roar** like other **bears.**

Not the best eyesight.

Famously **too lazy** to create many baby **pandas.**

Spends up to **12 hours a day asleep,** and the remaining **12, chomping bamboo.**

Only eats plants yet somehow remains **chunky.**

Six digits on forepaws.

Poops around 62 pounds (28 kg) of ~~barnpoo~~ bamboo each day. Ouch.

Five down the back.

Baby pandas are born bright pink, deaf, and blind. They pop out at only 6 inches (15 cm) long and weigh just 3.5 ounces (100 g). Luckily, female pandas make marvelous mothers and take great care of their little ones for around 18 months. By munching vast quantities of bamboo (and very little else), baby pandas quickly grow up to 5 feet (1.5 m) long, and can weigh a whopping 298 pounds (135 kg) by the time they reach maturity around six years old.

Giraffe weevil.

Bugus neckus ridiculum.

A male giraffe weevil
has a distinctly longer
neck than a female.
The ladies are the
lesser of two weevils. →

In the winter, it
has trouble finding →
scarves that fit.

Can fly!
Although looks
a bit awkward
mid-air.

No sting. →

No bite.

← Can you guess how
these weevils
got their name?

The long neck is
← primarily used for
fighting rival males.
Please note: necks are
not the best weapon.

← Female giraffe weevils
will often referee
fighting males!

← No pincers.

These fussy little beetles choose to live in only one place (Madagascar)
and in one specific tree—the giraffe beetle tree! Female giraffe weevils
use the soft, hairy leaves of their preferred trees to create a cocoon,
in which they lay their eggs.

Pink fairy armadillo.

~~Chlamyphorus truncatus.~~

Fairyflossius terrashrimpy.

These frilly bits are a vain attempt to look fancy (they also help gauge distance by feeling their surroundings).
↓

Protective armor in the toughest of all the colors— baby pink.

Poor eyesight.

Absurdly huge front claws for showing off, and also tunneling.

Not-so-huge rear claws for moving along and/or awkwardly high-fiving the armadillo behind.

The smallest of the armadillo family are also known as "sand swimmers." These tiny tunnelers are one of the few land mammals that don't have visible external ears (therefore you'll never catch one wearing sunglasses). Not that they would need sunglasses, as they spend most of their lives underground, munching on invertebrates as well as the odd plant root. Lovely.

Terrible **pet.**
↓

At only 4.3 inches (11 cm) long, pink fairy armadillos are incredibly cute, but they are also particularly susceptible to stress. They do not fare too well in captivity—most meet their end within a week. So no petting!

To escape predators (and pet shop owners), pink fairy armadillos can submerge themselves in sand very quickly. Once underground, they curl up and their shell acts as a cork to block the entrance to the burrow.

↑
So defensive...

Very serious disclaimer:
Contrary to their **name** (and this highly questionable illustration), pink fairy armadillos **do not have wings.** Or wands. Nor will they reward you for a lost tooth.

Pink fairy armadillos have evolved over many millennia to live a strictly nocturnal lifestyle—only operating under the cover of darkness. Just like the tooth fairy.

Parrotfish.

~~Scaridae.~~ Excrementus exfoliatus.

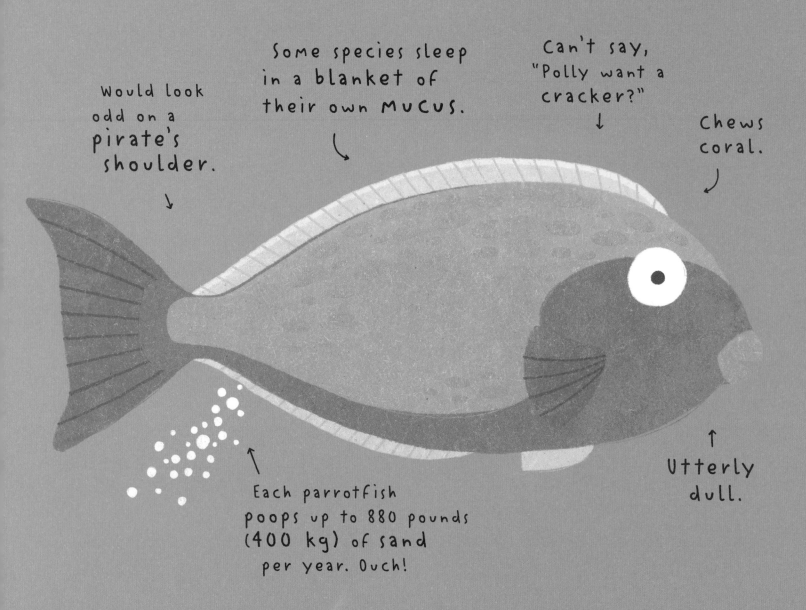

Would look odd on a **pirate's shoulder.** ↓

Some species sleep in a blanket of their own MUCUS. ↓

Can't say, "Polly want a cracker?" ↓

Chews coral. ↓

Each parrotfish poops up to 880 pounds (400 kg) of sand per year. Ouch! ↑

↑ Utterly dull.

This large fishy family is named after their fused front teeth, which look like parrot beaks and are used to scrape algae and invertebrates from coral. As they crunch around for their lunch, parrotfish bite off large chunks of rock-hard coral. To ensure they get all of the goodness from each gritty mouthful, parrotfish have a second set of teeth at the back of their mouths, which they use to crush the unwanted bits of coral into tiny pieces. The parrotfish will spit out any excess rubble and poop out the remainder! Over millennia, this sandy secretion builds up on the beaches close to coral reefs. So next time you get to play on a white, sandy beach, just consider where that sand came from.

Sugar glider.

~~Petaurus breviceps.~~

Furreus icarus.

Male sugar gliders
get **bald spots!**

Sweet tooth!
Loves a bit of
nectar, honey,
and even **sap.**

Wannabe
flying
squirrel.

↑
Extremely
sharp little
claws.

↑
Can you imagine
having **giant**
flaps of **skin**
that **connect**
your **wrists** and
ankles?

Sugar gliders are kept
as **pets** in homes
around the world,
where they take
great **joy** in
peeing on sofas.

These arboreal marsupials are beautifully adapted for life in the trees.
Their patageum (wing-like folds of skin) allow them to glide between
trees for up to 148 feet (45 metres). When they land, an opposable toe
on each hind foot is ideal for grabbing and climbing the tree. Their ankles
can rotate up to 180 degrees, which allow these little tree huggers to climb
down tree trunks, head first. While they look very similar, sugar gliders
bear no close relation to the flying squirrel.

Capuchin monkey.

~~Cebus imitator.~~

Peepee stinkipaws.

Smelly ~ hands.

A smashing → rock.

↗ Able to use simple tools (though tools pick up a yellowish tinge from pee-covered paws).

Hairy armpits. ↗

Jungle tuxedo.

Has never won an Academy Award, and most probably never will.

These piddling primates are thought to be the smartest of all the new world monkeys (those that live in Central and South America). They use tools, such as flat-sided rocks, to crack nuts, shells, and seeds, and they use thin sticks to fish ants and termites out of their nests.

They are highly social little creatures, communicating with their primate pals through a complex series of sounds, physical gestures, and facial expressions. Just like us! In fact, capuchins are so similar to us that in the 1920s and 1930s they were dressed as jockeys and made to ride racing greyhounds. Poor creatures. These days, you will see them in heaps of Hollywood movies.

I didn't sign up for this.

Not a
qualified
jockey.

Occupied.

But they're not all glitz and glamor. Male capuchins regularly pee on their hands and use the urine to wash their feet. It's not clear why, but it may be to attract a mate or let other capuchins know what's what.

Tufted deer.

~~Elaphodus cephalophus.~~

Dracularis barkus bambi.

Why is this deer named after this little tuft of fur...

Woof! This deer barks like a dog when agitated. →

Their tail has a dark side. ↓

↑ ...and not after its terrifyingly humongous Fangs?

↑ All bark no bite.

↑ Coarse fur (no petting).

Despite their vampire-like appearance, tufted deer are strict herbivores and spend much of their day grazing on grasses, shrubs, and fruit. Tufted deer escape from danger by wagging their tails up and down as they run. When the tail points up, the light underside of the tail is visible to predators, but when down, the dark top side of the tail shows. This simple strategy confuses predators, and helps the deer make a clean getaway.

Treehopper.

~~Membracidae.~~

Thorneus oucheus.

The scientific word for this pointy bit is the pronotum.

The common word used when you sit on one is not fit to print.

Aren't bushes **prickly** enough without insects pretending to be thorns?

← Also known as thorn bugs.

A group of thorn bugs is called a "bramble." Joke.

Only lives for a few months.

Many cultures believe that if you are **prickly** in this lifetime, you will come back next as a thorn bug.

These sharply dressed insects are masters of disguise. While perched on the stem of a plant, their pointy exoskeleton perfectly mimics the shape of a sharp thorn, camouflaging the bug to predators. There are over 3,200 species of treehopper and they can be found on every continent, except Antarctica (so watch out next time you sit on a log or a tree stump!).

Coconut crab.

~~Birgus latro.~~

Pinchiae pinchius.

Pretentious **moustache.**

A bit **pinchy.**

Shifty eyes.

Yoink!

Crabby demeanor.

↑ Totally nuts for **coconuts.**

↑ Also known as the **"robber crab"** (it will steal your stuff).

↑ **"Cop crabs"** are so far unknown to science.

Coconut crabs have an incredible sense of smell, which they use to locate food. However, this superpower can also get them into trouble with humans. Curious coconut crabs will follow their noses into people's homes, hotel rooms, beach bags, and backpacks to explore any new smells.

Once they find the smelly new thing—be it rubbish, food, or even a camera—coconut crabs often grab the swag with their prolific pincers, and escape with it! This is such a common occurrence that they are nicknamed "robber crabs."

You'll find a coconut crab pretty much anywhere you find coconut palms—all around the Indian and central Pacific Oceans. And you've guessed it, they love to eat coconuts! These three-foot-long (1-m) crustaceans have evolved claws large and powerful enough to crack through a coconut shell without breaking a sweat.

Leafy seadragon.

~~Phycodurus eques.~~

Folium fancypants.

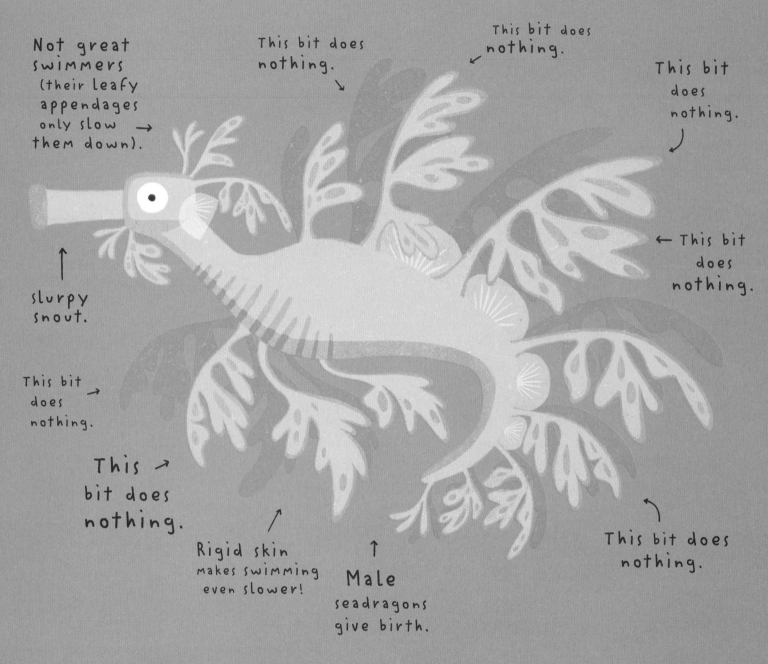

Not great swimmers (their leafy appendages only slow them down). →

This bit does nothing. ↓

This bit does nothing. ←

This bit does nothing. ↓

← This bit does nothing.

↑ slurpy snout.

This bit does nothing. →

This → bit does nothing.

Rigid skin makes swimming even slower! ↑

↑ Male seadragons give birth.

This bit does nothing. ↑

These incognito cousins of the seahorse float amongst seaweed, along the southern coast of Australia. Their fancy disguise is so elaborately evolved to resemble its surroundings that the leafy seadragon has no known predators. And just like seahorses, male leafies can warm their partners' eggs beneath their tails. The mother seadragon will lay her eggs into the father's pouch during mating, where the eggs will sit for up to nine weeks. Once they are ready to hatch, hundreds of little leafies will make their way into the blue.

Gentoo penguin.

~~Pygoscelis papua.~~

Waddlus tux romanticus.

3% of ice in Antarctica is frozen penguin pee! (They've been peeing there for at least 60 million years.)

Poor eyesight on land. →

Can't fly. ↘

← Toothless.

↗ No idea what "gentoo" means, or where the name came from.

↑ Despite living in Antarctica, a Gentoo will only breed in areas free from snow and ice. Picky.

↖ Sheds all of its feathers once a year, in what is known as a "catastrophic molt"!

The third-largest species of penguin in the Antarctic, gentoos use small rocks and pebbles to build their nests. Male gentoos also often offer up rocks as gifts, in an effort to win the affection of a female. While they may waddle around a little ungracefully on land, these penguins are incredibly well adapted to life in the water. They can swim faster than any other bird, at over 22 miles (35 km) per hour, and can hold their breath for up to 7 minutes! Even their eyes work better underwater than they do on land.

Leafcutter ant.

~~Atta cephalotes.~~

Chompi chompi nibbleologist.

Can strip a tree of all its **leaves** within **24 hours.** Poor tree! ↓

Carries leaves back and **forth** all day, like a sap. ↳

Never takes a **day off** (probably a bit stressed). ↓

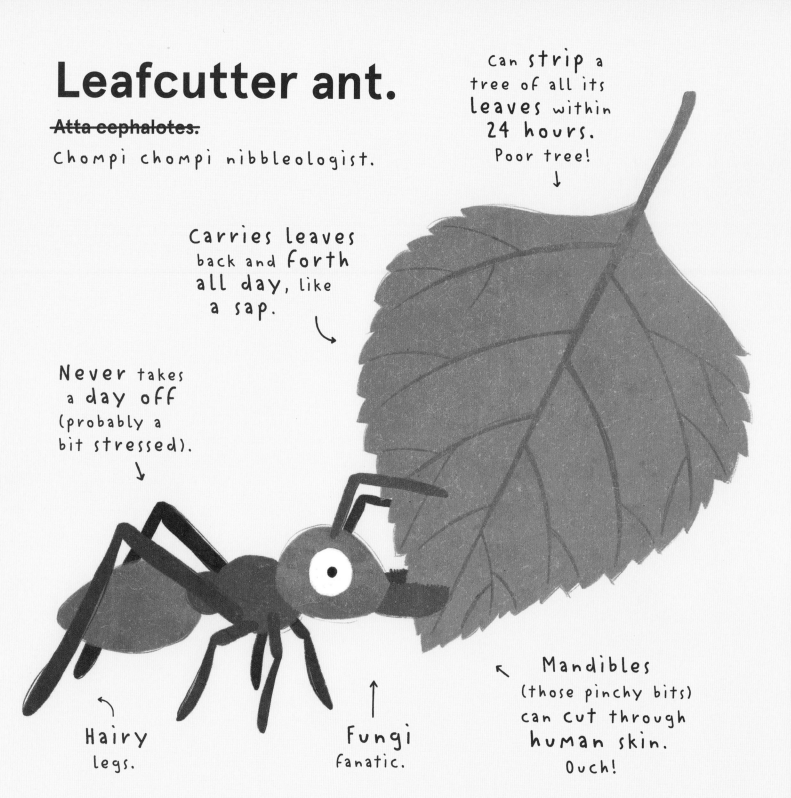

Hairy legs. ↲

Fungi fanatic. ↑

↖ **Mandibles** (those pinchy bits) can cut through **human skin.** Ouch!

These industrious insects are famed for their ability to snip and carry large pieces of plant. But leafcutter ants don't eat the leaves, instead they take them back to their nest, where the leaves decay. Fungi grow on the decaying leaves and the ants feast on the fungi. Like all species of ant, leafcutters perform an essential ecological role. Through their tireless work, leafcutter ants help to regenerate and enrich the soil around them, which allows new life to grow. Apart from humans, leafcutters form the most complex societies on Earth, with highly organized colonies supporting up to 10 million ants!

Giraffe.

~~Giraffa camelopardalis.~~

Camelopardis
ridiculus.

Only sleeps for around half an hour each night (that's how long it takes them to get their head down).

No vocal → cords.

Has to do the splits to take a drink!

Sleeps standing up.

Female giraffes ← give birth standing up!

Male giraffes drink female giraffe's pee to determine mating time.

Not giraffe pee (but the frog may have...).

Giraffes are pretty magnificent. They are the tallest land animals on Earth, reaching heights of up to 19 feet (5.8 m) (that's taller than three adult humans)! However, a giraffe's height doesn't always work in its favor. Despite their long necks, giraffes have to strike a very awkward pose just to get a drink of water! Luckily, they don't drink too often—only once every few days—as they get most of their water from leaves.

The world's snaggliest **snaggletooth!**
↙

Unlike most whales, it **never leaves** the icy, cold waters of the **Arctic.** Brrr!
↓

↑
Looks **a bit scary,** but is very sensitive.

Tusk grows through the upper lip. Ouch!

No teeth (other than → the obvious)!

Narwhal.

~~Monodon monoceros.~~

Gnarleus megatoothface.

The narwhal's mythical-looking "horn" is actually a modified tooth that grows through the upper jaw. Most male narwhals have a single tusk—which can grow up to 10 feet (3 m) long—but occasionally males will grow two. Female narwhals can also develop a tusk, although this is far more rare. The tusk is packed with millions of nerves, so it is incredibly sensitive. It's not known what it is used for, but it is likely that the tusk plays a role in locating food, and impressing the ladies (similar to the way male peacocks flash their feathers).

Narwhals don't have a dorsal fin so they use their whole body to break sea ice when they need to come up for air. However, they can hold their breath for as long as 25 minutes! Narwhals use this skill to dive for food—and they can go deep, down to depths of 4,900 feet (1,500 m), in search of the softest squid, fish, and shrimp. Narwhals don't have any teeth in their mouths, and feed by sucking in unsuspecting sea creatures, like an enormous high-powered vacuum.

No dorsal fin.

Narwhals have a few nicknames—they are famously known as the "Unicorn of the sea." Can't see why.

Its Inuit name, "Qilalugaq qirniqtaq" means "the one that points to the sky."

"Narwhal" is derived from Old Norse—"nar" meaning "corpse"—as they thought the whales looked like the bloated bodies of sunken sailors.

Chinchilla.

~~Chinchillidae.~~

Likesit chilleus.

Will overheat and **self-destruct** in the **heat** of your living room.
↓

Takes **dust baths!** Seems a little counter-productive? ↵

Teeth **never stop** growing! ↓

Supersensitive hearing means it can **startle** easily, which can cause it to **spray pee** at you. ↵

Grows up to **75 hairs** from every follicle! ↑

May be a chubby squirrel in a fancy fur coat. ↵

These adorably soft rodents can thrive at high altitudes, where the air is thin and cold (as low as 23°F (-5°C)!). Over millions of years, chinchillas have evolved a very dense coat of fine, smooth fur to help stay warm. Their soft coat and social nature means chinchillas are highly prized as pets, and they are often exported to climates far warmer than they're used to. So when kept indoors, the chinchilla's luxurious fur commonly causes them to overheat and pop their furry little clogs.

Hummingbird hawk-moth.

~~Macroglossum stellatarum.~~

Papilio incognito.

Terrifyingly **dusty** ← wings.

DIY pipe cleaner antennae! (An easy Halloween costume idea.)

Proboscis can be the whole length, ← or **longer**, of its body. That's just **showing off.**

↑ **Sweet tooth.**

↑ **Look** at all of that **fuzz!** Must get **a bit warm** in the **summer.**

↑ **Hums** because it doesn't know the words.

The impressively strong wings of this marvelous moth can beat 70 times per second, allowing it to hover around its favorite food so it can use its tongue-like proboscis to suck the nectar from flowering plants. Just like its namesake, the hummingbird, this supermoth hums as it hovers. But these bugs bear no relation to the bird—instead the pair are a wonderful example of convergent evolution, where two separate species have evolved similar behaviors (and a similar appearance) to make the most of their environment.

Zooplankton.

Vivus soupus.

Just drifts along, waiting to be Munched. →

Lives in the ocean but can't really swim. ↓

Zooplankton can be microscopic, but many are visible to the naked eye. The group includes tiny jellyfish, crustaceans (such as krill), fish eggs, larvae, gastropods, and many, many, many more.

Plankton are organisms that drift along in the upper layers of the ocean. There are two types of plankton: phytoplankton, which are microscopic plant organisms, and zooplankton, which are animals that feed on other plankton.

I think this one flew out when a **dolphin sneezed.** ↓

Is this one a **Sea Monkey?** ↳

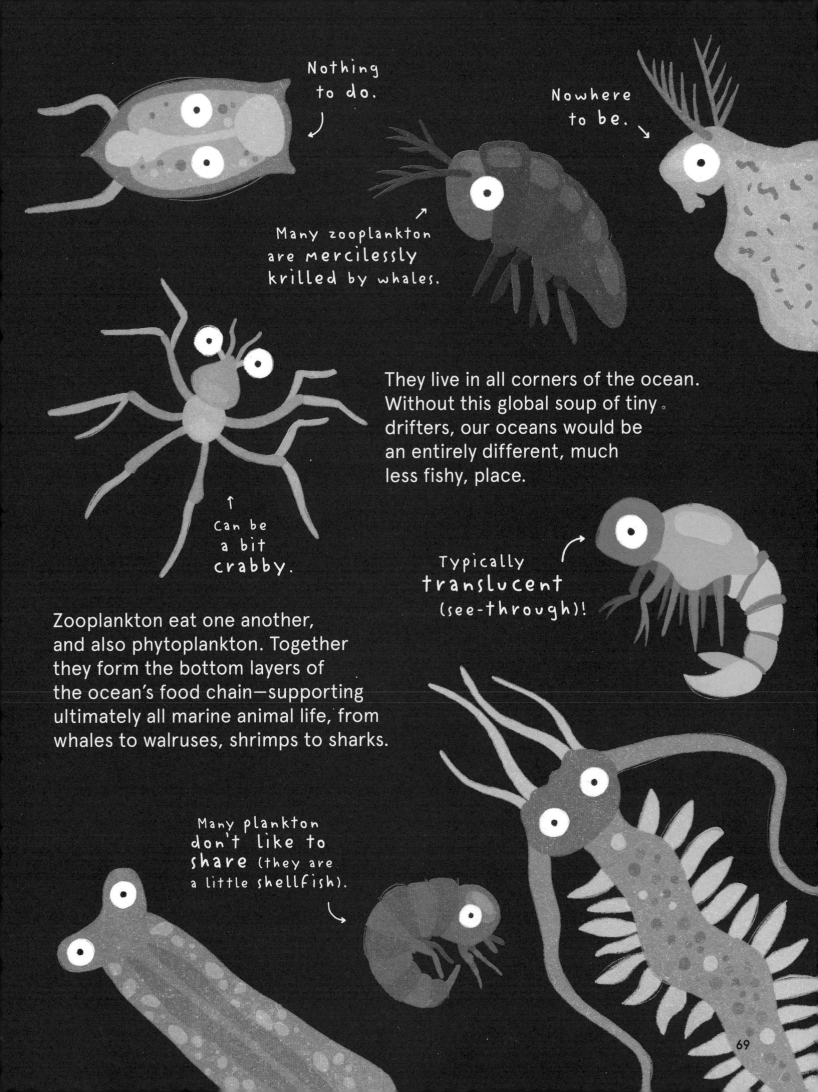

Nothing
to do.

Nowhere
to be.

Many zooplankton
are mercilessly
krilled by whales.

They live in all corners of the ocean.
Without this global soup of tiny
drifters, our oceans would be
an entirely different, much
less fishy, place.

↑
Can be
a bit
crabby.

Typically
translucent
(see-through)!

Zooplankton eat one another,
and also phytoplankton. Together
they form the bottom layers of
the ocean's food chain—supporting
ultimately all marine animal life, from
whales to walruses, shrimps to sharks.

Many plankton
**don't like to
share** (they are
a little shellfish).

Dumbo octopus.

~~Grimpoteuthis.~~

Cuteus octopi.

This family of deep-sea, deeply cute cephalopods are instantly recognizable for their elephant ear-like fins that stick out from the sides of their mantle (the part that looks like a head). Just as the flying elephant in the movie used his ears to get around, dumbo octopuses flap their ear-like fins to get from A to B.

Extra fins (are eight arms not enough?).

Swallow food whole! → It would probably put all eight elbows on the table too. (If it had elbows.)

Blue blood (no relation to the Royal Family... that we know of).

Huge eyes (about one third the width of its head), yet eyesight is very poor.

Can't squirt ink, unlike many octopuses.

Part of a family known as "umbrella octopuses." So be careful not to put one up indoors.

Nine brains.

Three hearts!

To move at a faster pace, dumbo octopuses pump their umbrella-like arms in unison. Although, they rarely need to make a quick getaway. They live at such extreme depths (at least 2.5 miles (4 km) below sea level), that it's unusual to encounter hungry predators.

Elephant shrew.

~~Macroscelididae.~~

Leapus trunkface elonmuskybutt.

Shrew-like
expression.
↓

Also known as the
"jumping shrew"
(easily frightened).
↓

Pee-ew! A gland beneath
the tail produces a MUSKY
scent to mark territory
and put off predators.
↓

Not a
trunk.
↓

↑
Definitely not
an elephant.

Word of warning:
never try to tame
this shrew, unless
you like your
pets musky.
↗

↑
Not a real
shrew.

↖ Slightly
creepy,
scaly tail.

Also known by its African name sengi, elephant shrews are typically less than 6 inches (15 cm) long, but can jump about 3 feet (1 m) in the air! This behavior helps them avoid their many predators (such as snakes and large lizards). Elephant shrews mate for life, but spend most of their time alone, searching for ants, grubs, and tasty termites with their impressive trunk-like snouts.

Mosquito.

~~Culicidae.~~

Annoyus maxiumus.

will fly up to 13.6 miles (22 km) for a blood meal!

Only female mosquitos will drink your blood!

Humanity's greatest predator.

Hunts by sensing the carbon dioxide we exhale.

"Bites" can cause terrible itchiness.

Male mosquitos don't suck your blood (they are vegan, feeding on plant nectar alone).

Females can carry up to three times their own body weight in blood.

The world's most deadly animal is not a lion, a snake, a reconstituted velociraptor, or even an angry hippo...it's a mosquito! The mosquito carries a whole host of vile viruses, which cause deadly diseases such as malaria and dengue fever. As a result they've been responsible for the loss of more human lives than any other animal. Yet as annoying and dangerous as they are to us humans, only a few species of mosquito actually drink blood, and fewer still prefer to prey upon humans—many pounce on birds, frogs, and other creatures. The world's 3,000 plus species of mosquito perform an essential role as food for larger insects, mammals, reptiles, and birds.

Aardvark.

~~Orycteropus afer.~~

Aalphabetum primis.

Eaars.

Aardvarks are notorious vowel hogs.

Baack.

Did Mother Nature feel guilty for cobbling a creature together from spare parts?

☐ Pig snout.
☐ Rabbit ears.
☐ Kangaroo tail.

Thick skin (looks like it needs it).

Taail.

Color-blind.

Can't burrow in rocky soil (it's too aard).

Lives in a hole.

Stumpy legs.

These African mammals live almost exclusively on insects. And they eat a lot of them! Aardvarks use their stocky legs and powerful claws to dig into termite nests, munching up to 50,000 termites every night! The termites aren't so keen on becoming the victims of such an atrocity, so they bite back. However, the aadvark has a couple of tricks up its furry sleeve—they have evolved incredibly thick skin to resist the malicious mandibles of biting termites. Better still, they can close their nostrils at will, to stop termites getting in!

Garden snail.

~~Cornu aspersum.~~ Slimeus spiralis domus.

Some snails greet one another with an eye-five.

Moves at a snail's pace: top speed 0.028 miles (0.045 km) per hour!

No backbone.

Despite their quiet appearance, many snails are unruly cannibals!

No teeth.

Leaves a slimy trail of mucus.

Just a slug with a shell?

A snail is considered a culinary delicacy in many cultures around the world.

Some people even eat snail eggs *gross*. They call the dish "white caviar."

Snails belong to a highly successful family known as gastropods—of which there are around 43,000 species. Over an astonishing 500 million years, they have adapted to live almost everywhere, from deep in the ocean to dry, dusty deserts. And they come in all sizes—from less than 1 mm in length (small enough to fit through the eye of a needle), up to a whopping 15.3 inches (39 cm) long! Snails play an important ecological role—breaking down vegetation and propping up food chains, wherever they slowly crawl.

Golden poison frog.

~~Phyllobates terribilis.~~ Croakus croakus.

This coloring is Mother Nature's way of saying...

"Do not lick this frog!"

(You will croak if you do.)

Eats whatever bugs it. ↓

Feeds its tadpoles its own eggs. Sunny side up. ↙

Poison is produced in the skin. ↓

↖ No teeth or spines to deliver poison.

↖ Generally relies on being eaten to teach its attacker a lesson. (This ends well for neither party.)

↑ Warning! Do not eat!

↖ Bright yellow is not the best camouflage.

As you might have guessed by its unambiguous name, this little amphibian is considered to be one of the most toxic creatures on the planet. At only the height of a paper clip, each individual packs enough poison to take down ten human adults! Because of its ability to produce such lethal toxins, the golden poison dart frog has only one predator—the also appropriately named fire-bellied snake. There are over 200 species of poison dart frogs in their native forests of South America, where they evolved around 45 million years ago (and have been living, sensibly undisturbed, ever since).

Kiwi.

~~Apteryx mantelli.~~

Nonflightius nonfruitius.

Not related to kiwi fruit, although it is somewhat similar in appearance.

Almost completely blind.

Perhaps it's green in the middle?

Cannot fly (puny wings).

Why does this bird have whiskers?

Scruffy feathers.

Heavy bones.

These tiny flightless birds are native to New Zealand. People there are so infatuated by them, they call themselves "Kiwis." Their small size (the birds, not the people), soft fur-like feathers, and cat-like whiskers make these peculiar birds particularly adorable. Kiwis are the only bird with nostrils at the end of their beaks, which they use to forage for food. Their sense of smell is excellent, which compensates for their not-so-excellent eyesight. To top off this compendium of cuteness, kiwis are incredibly shy, which may be why they are nocturnal. Oh, and they mate for life.

Axolotl.

~~Ambystoma mexicanum.~~

Pinkius pointless gilli gilli.

Unnecessarily extravagant gills.

Young axolotls eat each other. Not so cute!

Can't blink. No eyelids!

Doesn't chew its food — simply sucks it in. Rude.

Eats tadpoles. Yummy.

Has to swallow stones to help digest food.

Dances a little waltz to initiate mating, just like your great-grandfather did.

Native to just one freshwater river system in Mexico, these amazing amphibians can breathe underwater through their branching gills, or on land through their lungs (although this is rare). But even more remarkable is the axolotl's ability to regenerate body parts following an injury. They can regrow limbs, their tail, eyes, even broken spines and damaged brains, perfectly—time and time again.

In closing.

The creatures in this book do not have any place to be, or any particular point to prove. They are here (just as we are here) quite by accident, to experience our wonderful world. They remind us that while we are all very different, no matter who we are, there is a place for each and every one of us. We are all made from the same stuff, we all share the same planet, and we are a part of the same whole.

Ha-ha.
↓

Yep—you, me, platypus, plankton, and pufferfish—we are all on different branches of the same family tree, one that goes back to the very first life on Earth. So, it is up to every one of us to respect and look after the people and other animals we share our planet with. Most of the time, this simply means letting each other be. Even the pink fairy armadillo? But they are so cu... *Especially* the pink fairy armadillo.

Index.

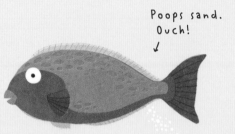
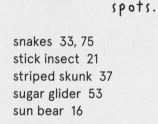